Celebrating the Centenary, 1977

By Bertha Natanielu

Illustrated by Mila Aydingoz

We respect and honour Aboriginal and Torres Strait Islander Elders past, present and future. We acknowledge the stories, traditions and living cultures of Aboriginal and Torres Strait Islander peoples on this land and commit to building a brighter future together.

Library For All Ltd.

2

My family is from the Torres Strait Islands, but I was born and raised in Cairns. I grew up with the Aboriginal kids there.

I didn't want to claim myself as Torres Strait Islander until I was older. I was curious about my culture and Island home.

When I was 22 years old, I decided it was time to go for a holiday to my island home. That was in 1975.

As soon as the plane landed on Horn Island, I fell in love with the bright blue water. I had never seen water so beautiful.

Where we lived in Cairns was on the mudflats, so the water was a dark brown.

I was so excited. I decided I would stay and never go back to Cairns.

I got a job working at the Federal Hotel as a pantry maid.

Then, in 1977, we had the Torres Strait Island Centenary.

All of the defence force were up there celebrating.

The streets were alive with activities!
Everyone was dancing and singing to
celebrate our culture.

One of the activities was a charity pageant. It was called 'Queen of Pearls', and it raised money for the Heart Foundation. My friends entered me into the pageant, and they made me a beautiful dress.

I had to walk down the runway with a Navy escort.

I raised $50 000 dollars for the Heart Foundation that year, and I won the title of Charity Princess for raising the most money.

15

Since then, I have lived happily on Thursday Island with my family.

To this day, I continue to share my stories with my family about the historic moments I have enjoyed on the island.

The Torres Strait Island Centenary, 1977

The traditional custodians have lived in the Torres Strait Islands for thousands of years. But, during the 1850s, passing trading ships began stopping to explore the islands, discovering valuable sea cucumbers and pearls.

By the 1870s, there was a busy pearl industry growing in the Strait. Thursday Island was selected to be the regional administrative centre. An official government office was established there in 1877.

The Torres Strait Islands were annexed in 1879 to become part of the British Colony of Queensland. They became part of Australia in 1901, when Australia's states joined together in Federation.

In 1977, Thursday Island hosted a centenary event that was celebrated throughout the Torres Strait Islands. There were historical displays, cultural dancing and fundraising activities. A plaque and time capsule were laid. Many visitors, including representatives of the armed forces, visited the region.

Thursday Island resident Bertha Natanielu participated in the celebrations. This is her story about that time.

You can use these questions to talk about this book with your family, friends and teachers.

What did you learn from this book?

Describe this book in one word. Funny? Scary? Colourful? Interesting?

How did this book make you feel when you finished reading it?

What was your favourite part of this book?

About the author

Bertha Natanielu was born in Cairns but lives on Thursday Island, where she loves going camping with her friends and family. Bertha's favourite story as a child was *The Famous Five*, and her Our Yarning contributions are based off her own experiences.

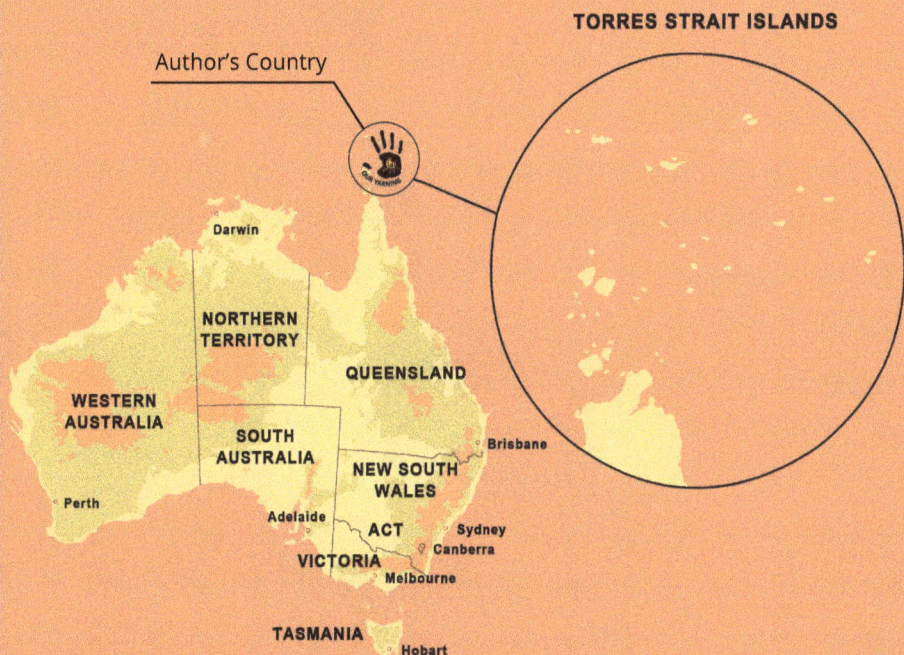

TORRES STRAIT ISLANDS

Author's Country

Darwin

NORTHERN
TERRITORY

QUEENSLAND

WESTERN
AUSTRALIA

SOUTH
AUSTRALIA

Perth

Adelaide

NEW SOUTH
WALES

Brisbane

ACT

Sydney
Canberra

VICTORIA

Melbourne

TASMANIA

Hobart

Our Yarning

The Our Yarning collection aligns with the Australian Curriculum through the Cross-Curriculum Priorities — Aboriginal and Torres Strait Islander Histories and Cultures. The collection provides an authentic opportunity for learning and embedding Aboriginal and Torres Strait Islander perspectives because it is written by Aboriginal and Torres Strait Islander people.

We know that children learn better, and enjoy reading more, when they see themselves in the stories, characters and illustrations of the books they read.

To download the app, visit the Google Play Store or Apple Store and search 'Our Yarning'.

librforyall.org

You're reading Middle Primary

Learner – Beginner readers
Start your reading journey with short words, big ideas and plenty of pictures.

Level 1 – Rising readers
Raise your reading level with more words, simple sentences and exciting images.

Level 2 – Eager readers
Enjoy your reading time with familiar words, but complex sentences.

Level 3 – Progressing readers
Develop your reading skills with creative stories and some challenging vocabulary.

Level 4 – Fluent readers
Step up your reading skills with playful narratives, new words and fun facts.

Middle Primary – Curious readers
Discover your world through science and stories.

Upper Primary – Adventurous readers
Explore your world through science and stories.

Celebrating the Centenary, 1977

First published 2024

Published by Library For All Ltd
Email: info@libraryforall.org
URL: libraryforall.org

Our Yarning logo design by Jason Lee, Bidjipidji Art

Original illustrations by Mila Aydingoz

Celebrating the Centenary, 1977
Natanielu, Bertha
ISBN: 978-1-923207-20-2
SKU04392